WILLIAM MORRIS

GLASS

ARTIFACT AND ART

Distributed by

University of Washington Press

Seattle & London

WILLIAM MORRIS

GLASS

ARTIFACT AND ART

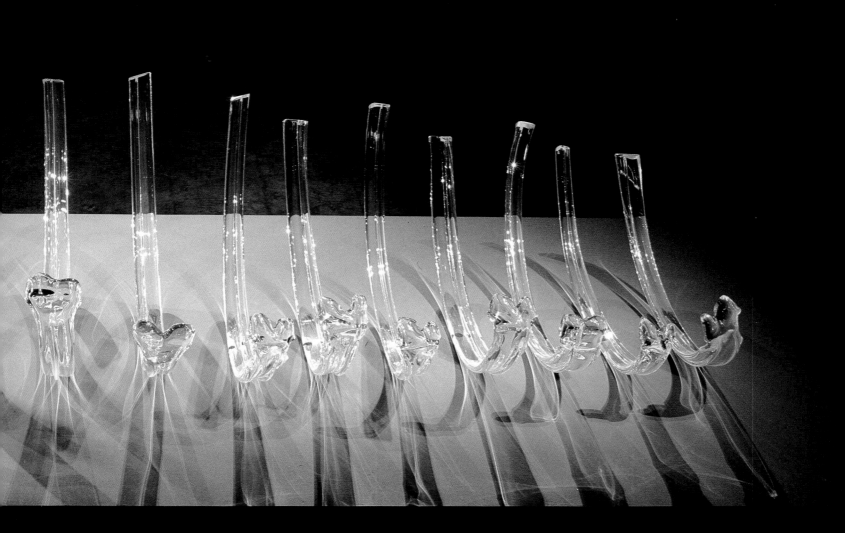

Installation, Brendan Walter Gallery, 1988.

Distributed by
University of Washington Press
P.O. Box 50096
Seattle, WA 98145

ISBN 0-295-96917-2

Printed in Japan.

Editor: Kate Elliott
Principal photographer: Robert Vinnedge
Designer: Katy Homans
Typesetter: Thomas & Kennedy
Printer: Nissha Printing

For further information about William Morris's work:
Brendan Walter Gallery
1001 Colorado Avenue
Santa Monica, CA 90401
and
Seventh at San Carlos
Carmel, CA 93921

cover:
Petroglyph Vessel, detail, 1988. See page 31, right.

On the following pages, height precedes width precedes depth. Works not available to the editors at the time of this publication have not been measured. Vessels average 15 to 28 inches high, Standing Stones 30 to 50 inches.

CONTENTS

THE STUBBORN VOICE FROM WITHIN

HENRY GELDZAHLER

William Morris's training as a glass artist has been exemplary. He has progressed with order and logic from neophyte to apprentice to journeyman. In the past five years he has become a master in his own right. His trajectory is startling and would have been unthought of in American glass before the pioneering efforts of the students of the legendary Harvey Littleton at the University of Wisconsin in the 1960s and 1970s. Among these it has been Dale Chihuly with whom Morris has been most closely associated. Indeed, William Morris first came to my attention as Chihuly's principal assistant and team leader, and it is in the face of Chihuly's prolificity of ideas about subject matter and materials that Morris has struck his own claim to such positive effect.

The nub of William Morris's personal esthetic is in the forest and earth — as opposed to Dale Chihuly's lifelong fascination with sea forms. Morris is a hunter who likes to pit himself against aspects of nature; it is death and its aftermath that haunts him and, through him, us. In this vein we find a recurring attention to cave men and women, to dinosaur footsteps and bones, to the general subject of cave paintings, sometimes referred to as petroglyphs. What is haunting about William Morris's work in glass is the constant accommodation he makes between his sense of the beautiful luminescence that is glass art's bane and its glory, and his identification with picturing the earth and its primordial verities. And it is this content in his pieces that in its starkness astonishes us. We are forced to feel and to think and to linger until they reveal their elegance and splendor.

Morris works in several veins at one time. It was with his large abstract volumetric pieces that I first came to know his work. In fact, when I helped in the purchase of artworks for the renovation of the Rainbow Room at Rockefeller Center it was in part due to a visual pun on skyscrapers that I suggested the purchase of his pieces then on view in a New York gallery.

It is in the Artifacts of 1988—89 that William Morris has found both his wittiest and starkest articulation. The glass bones and skulls distributed at random within a composition — as if that casualness expressed all that is left of the human-animal's poetry — are as moving to me as anything I have seen in contemporary glass art.

In fact the amazingly subtle and original visual sense that allows William Morris to create two skeletons, one white and one black, reaching toward and away from each other, reads to me as an ultimate paradigm of our national tragedy, racism.

It took Morris's Artifact #6 to make me realize such a simple, homely truth. All bones are white.

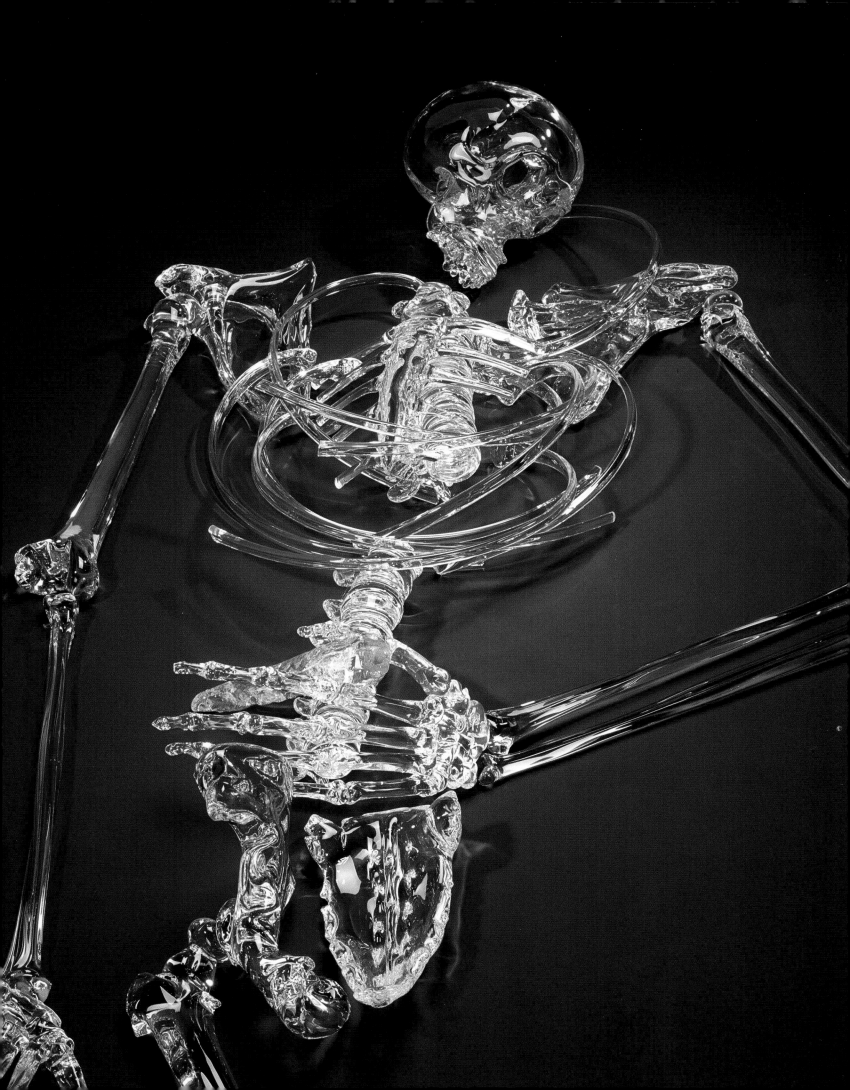

ARTIFACT AND ART

PATTERSON SIMS

William Morris's recent figurative sculpture in glass alternately suggests the worlds of Jean-Paul Sartre and Indiana Jones. Rarely has death looked so glamorous, bones glistened so elegantly, and narrative and meaning been so alluringly ambiguous. After many years of making vessels in glass that push craft, scale, color, and shape to virtuosic heights, in Morris's recent series of Artifacts he has turned to multi-boned, archaeological assemblages. As with the time warps of Indiana Jones's adventure fantasies, past and present, kitsch and truth, and portentuousness and wit are scrambled in Morris's recent pieces. These still lifes of bones offer a surreal and initially morbid twist on the accessible vessels that Morris's many admirers have come to expect. They express an intellectual and emotional depth never before visible in Morris's work; existential rumination is combined with picturesque escapism.

These new subjects first appeared in some of Morris's earliest work, when as a student at California State University at Chico, he made drawings of shaded and outlined human and animal bones on black paper. Morris soon abandoned this imagery to pursue the vessel form, briefly in the university's ceramics department and then in its fledgling studio glass program. Artifacts and the human figure fascinated him, but the physical allure and challenge of creating glass instantly made subject matter essentially irrelevent. It was not until 1988, following his thorough mastery of glass blowing and molding, that Morris would return to these themes in solid glass. Working with Venetian artisans, Morris mastered the techniques of thickening and coaxing molten glass into the heads, hands, and feet of his figures.

Drawn from his imagination and experience of nature, Morris's Artifact vignettes begin as small drawings. The process of creation is frenetic; Artifact #14 (Offering) was completed in two weeks. Morris's glass bones and skeletons are at once weighty and transparent, with the appearance of healthy, dimensional x-rays. They are distinctly muscular and fit, like Morris and his team. Morris's father, who is a doctor, observantly complains his son's glass bones are not anatomically correct. Overscaled and fleshy depictions of their subject, they repose in their beds of larger bones like the remains of certain ancient Pompeian victims, eternally frozen in postures of calm and even pleasure.

In Artifact #14 (Offering), glass thread pictographs (made by Morris's longtime friend, the sculptor Flora Mace) dance in a luminous, globular skull.

Morris's own dreams of hunting and pristine nature float in his skeletal alter ego. It is the ultimate idealized self-portrait. The elongated, yellow body is enveloped by an altar of blanched bones and clutches two vessels. Hollow and thin, the bones form a shelter that evokes a sunken boat, a mastodon, or (keyed to Jonas) a whale. This shelter exists in unity with the natural environment: a glass tomb that is sensuous, cool, and inviting, beyond the ravages of time.

It is not so surprising that Morris takes a clinical attitude toward the human body, and places it in a primordial setting. Morris's familiarity with the body and the life cycle begins with his solid medical background; in addition to his father's work, his mother and sister are nurses, his wife is a chiropractor, one brother is a doctor, and another is a biochemist. This family predilection was combined with a love of nature. Growing up in Carmel near the rugged Northern California coast, Morris went hiking, rock climbing, and camping frequently, first with his family and then alone. He recalls coming upon Indian burial sites and archaeological remains. Their impact, especially when he was alone, was profound. The experience is re-created in the new pieces. Morris took up hunting as soon as he could, partly as an excuse to wander in the woods. Hunting put him into a heightened relation to nature; it made him better able to understand its processes. Morris still hunts and prefers to do so alone. He now uses a bow and arrow and takes off the first month of hunting season as his only vacation.

Around 1986, animal and hunting motifs showed up on Morris's vessels. These first instances of representation were silhouetted against his vessels' mottled surfaces. Their depiction was loose, like ink blots that assumed shape. Male and female hunters and their quarry floated over glistening surfaces. Private and shamanistic, they resemble minute cave drawings.

These vessels were a bridge to Morris actually realizing these concerns sculpturally. His initial Artifacts grouped bone and shell-like fragments. They spilled forward, as if being freed or born from the vessels with which they were shown. For the series Morris created a new vessel type. First made of clear glass, his groupings were exhibited in spotlit darkness in stylish arrangements that simulate unearthed or robbed burial sites. Morris's growing technical finesse is evident from piece to piece. As they have grown more ambitious they have better succeeded in Morris's stated desire to "generate a story of situations of man, beast and nature not possible in the present."

For the first time in Morris's work, ideas have made an appearance. In his Standing Stone pieces, vague concepts of history and time were suggested, and in more recent vessels hunting narratives are rendered in more explicit and complex

terms. With the Artifacts Morris makes a conscious effort to break away from the world of craft and colorful interior design accents to which most glass vessels are consigned. He has moved beyond his own earlier work and that of most other studio glass artists who since the 1950s in America (and almost eternally in Venice) have been so pleased with what can be accomplished technically that they have otherwise neglected ideas and content. The pleasure and the routine of production and the appetites of the marketplace have generated extensive series of nearly identical works.

For too long the vessel has been both a refuge and a trap, and Morris with the Artifact series has done something significant in moving beyond the vessel to uncompromised sculpture. His melange in glass of archaeology and the apocalypse follows a period — from the mid-1970s to the mid-1980s — in which once again the human figure has been a central motif for advanced artists. But figuration since the 1970s has focused upon victims, the dead and the dying. AIDS, acid rain and ozone, and nuclear death and societal breakdown have been the points of reference. The human being has been seen at the vortex of surreal fantasy, misfortune, and disaster.

One can not think of Morris's bone pile-ups without recalling the earlier skeletal sculpture of Nancy Graves, Robert Morris (otherwise no relation) and Robert Arneson. William Morris is not the only sculptor in glass to use the figure to raise existential issues. Nancy Mee, Flora Mace and Joey Kirkpatrick, and Hank Murta Adams, among others, have also followed in the wake of the flood of figurative painting and sculpture that dominate recent art.

What these sculptors in glass lose by their delay, they gain in their choice of material. What better way to underscore the human figure's fragility and mortality than to use glass. Made in extreme heat, glass looks perennially cool. When used to invoke matters of death and darkness, it gleams with light and affirmation. Morris's view of death seems transcendent not final, radiant not extinguished. A glossy and slick medium has been imbued with content and pathos. William Morris's dealings with death have summoned forth his best work to date. He has turned artifacts into art.

left to right: Jon Ormbrek, Paul DeSomma, and William Morris casing Petroglyph Vessel with molten glass.

VESSELS

Roundel and Vessels with shard drawings, 1979.

Stone Vessel, 1984. 12 x 15 x 4½ inches.

Stone Vessel and Standing Stone, 1984.

Stone Vessel, 1984.

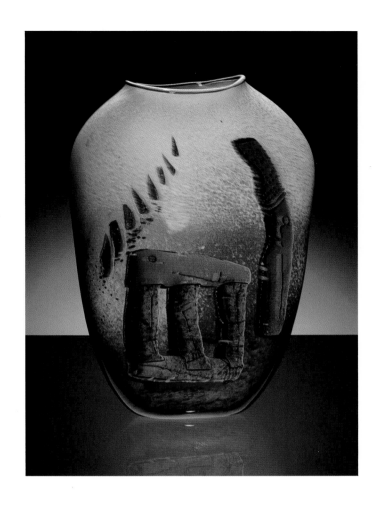

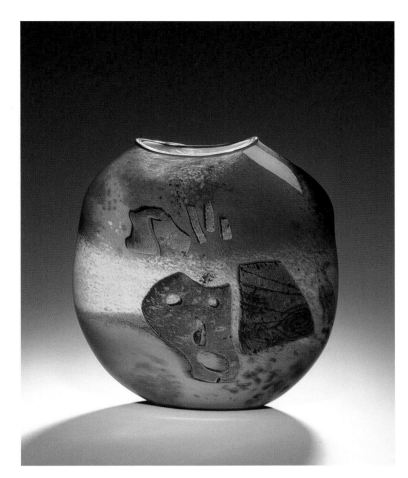

Stone Vessels, 1984–1986. 15 to 20 inches high.

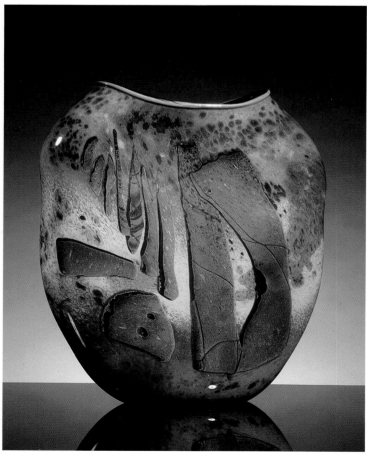

Stone Vessels, 1984–1986. 15 to 18 inches high.

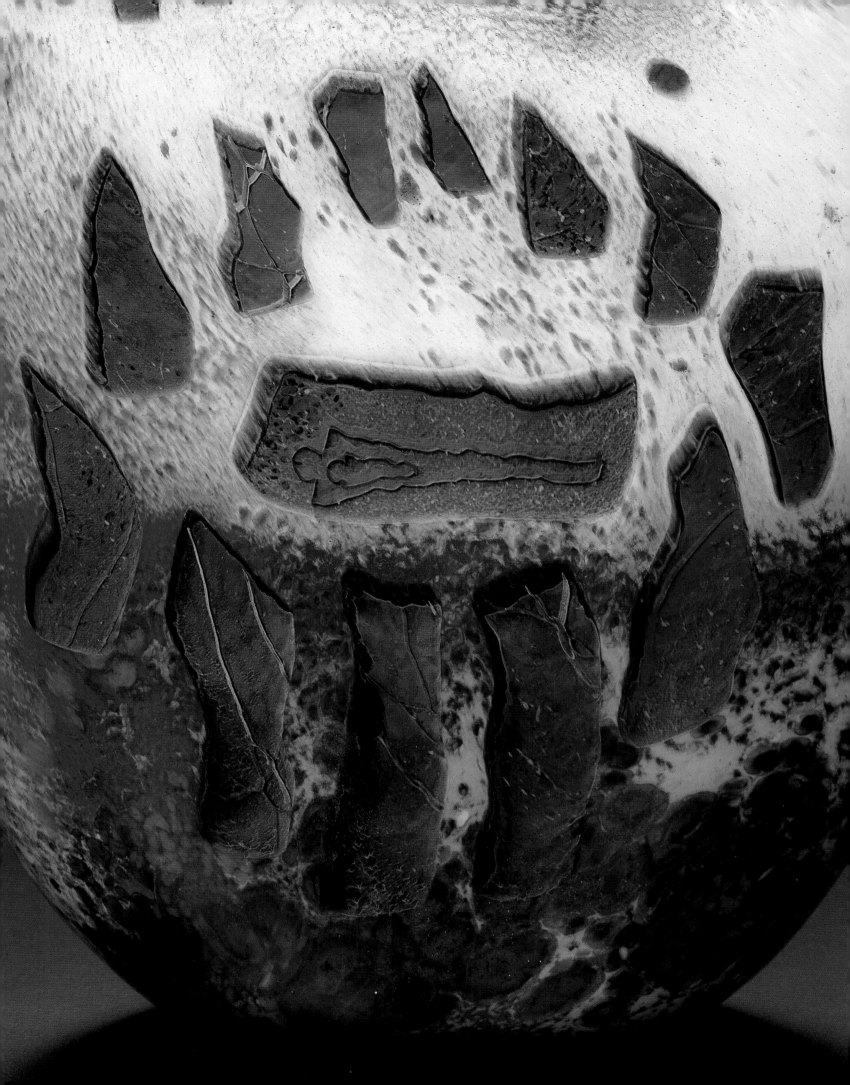

Standing Stone and Stone Vessel, detail, left, 1985.

Petroglyph Vessel, 1985.																	**Standing Stone, 1985. Petroglyph Vessel, reverse side of page 24.**

Petroglyph Vessel (Fighting Elks), detail left, 1988.

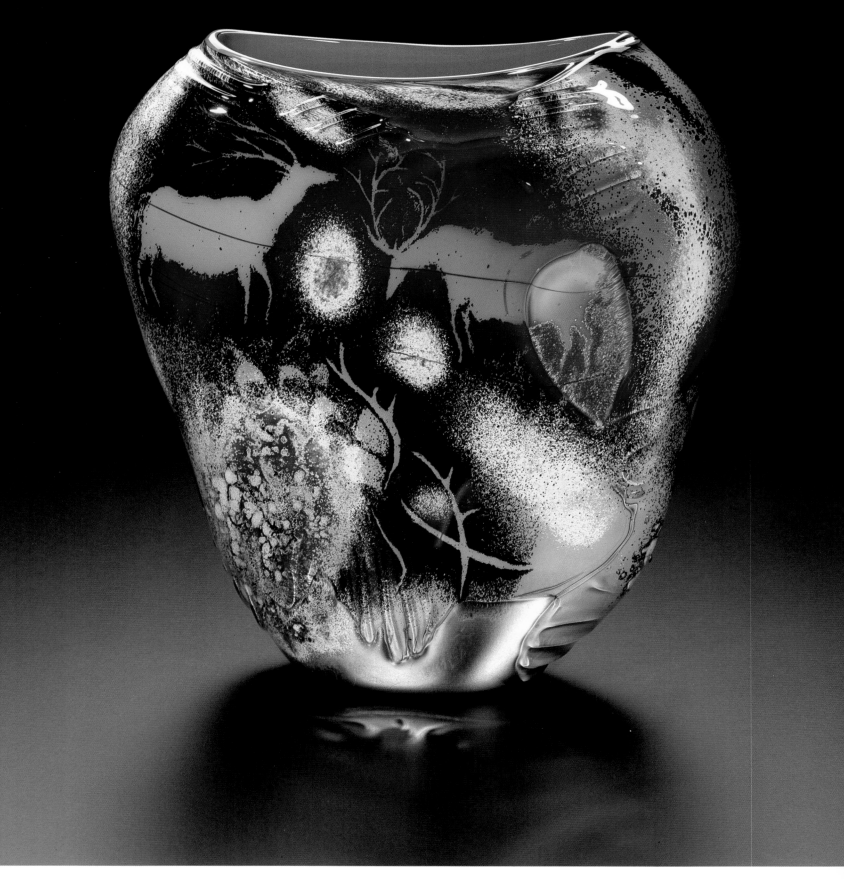

Petroglyph Vessel, 1988. 21 x 19 x 4½ inches. Both sides.

Petroglyph Vessels, 1988. 18 to 28 inches high.

following pages:

Petroglyph Vessel, 1988. Both sides.

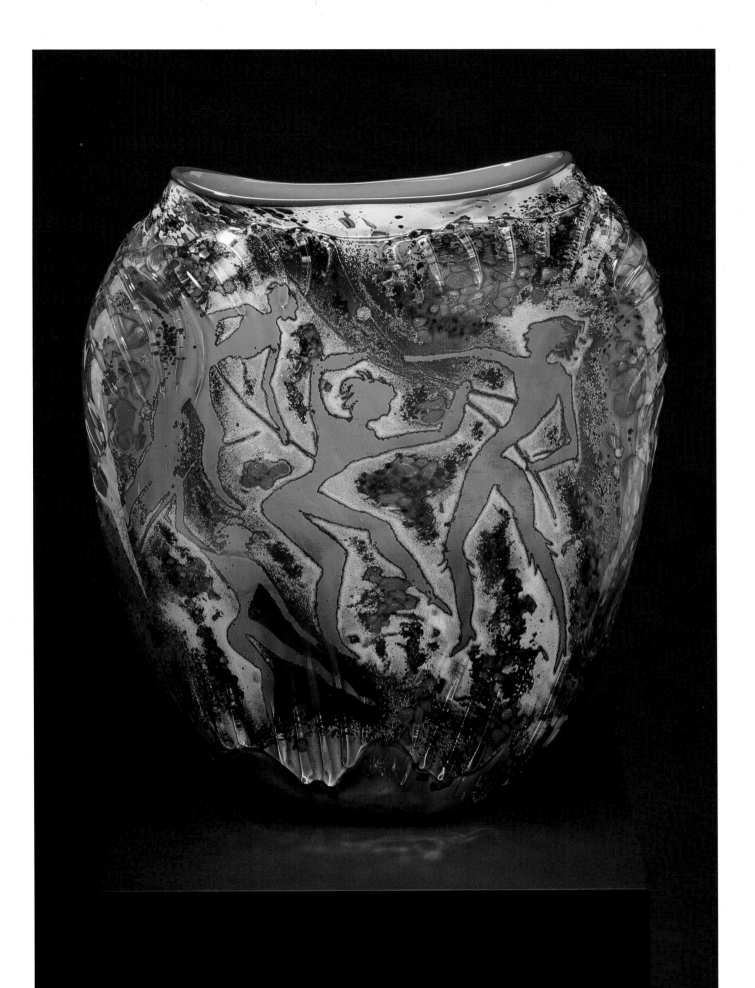

Petroglyph Vessel, 1988. Both sides.

Morris (top right), Jon Ormbrek, and Paul DeSomma releasing mold from a Standing Stone.

Standing Stone and Rocks, 1986. 33 x 30 x 24 inches.

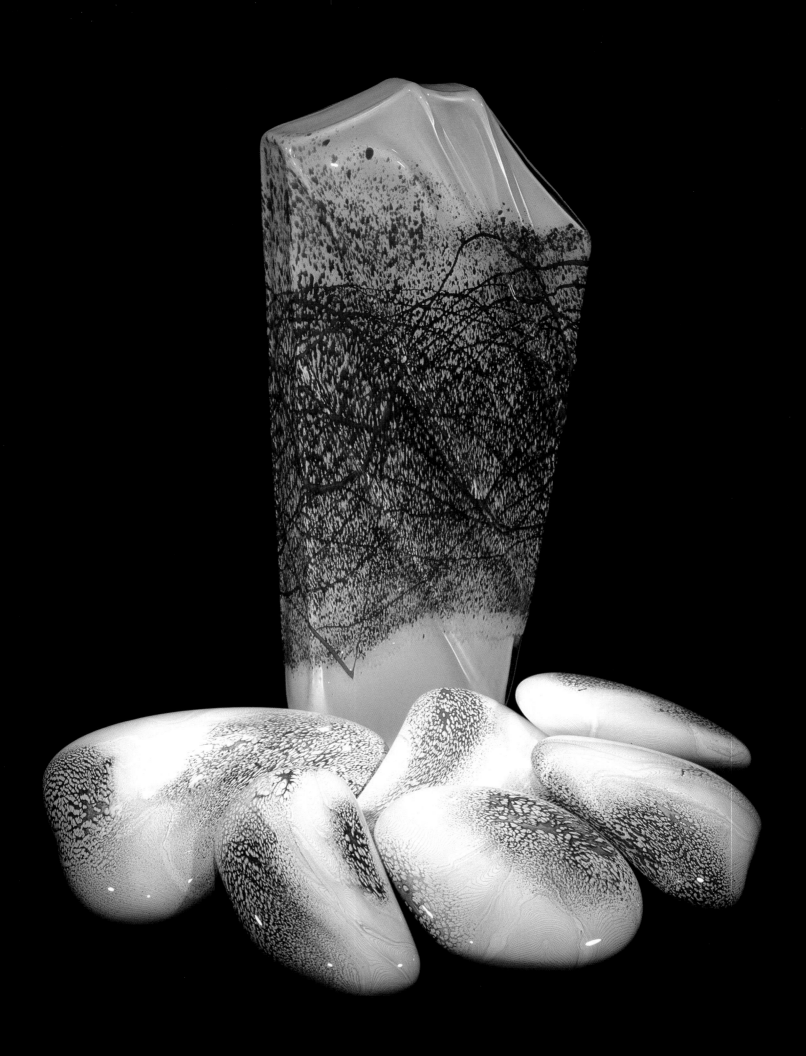

Rocks, 1986.

Vessel and Rocks, 1988. 21 x 36 x 30 inches.

following pages:

Standing Stone, 1983.

Standing Stone, 1984.

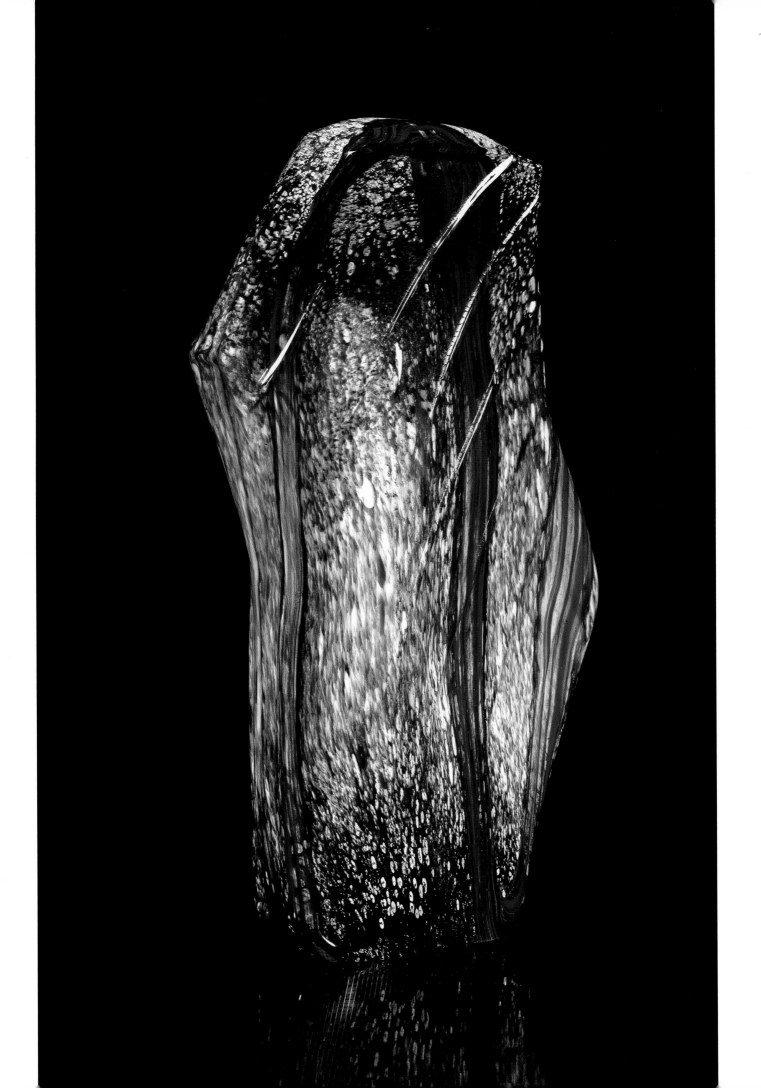

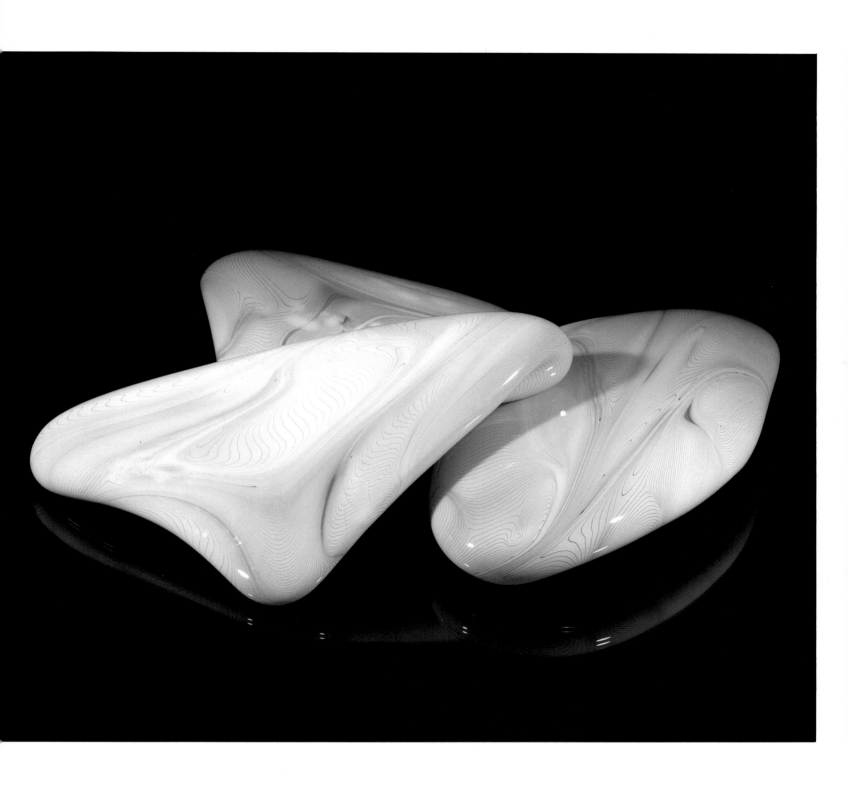

Rocks, 1987. 8 x 28 x 22 inches.

Vessel and Rocks, 1988.

following pages:

Standing Stone, 1985.

Standing Stones, 1987.

Standing Stone with Petroglyphs, 1987.

Standing Stone, 1989. 34 x 19 x 7 inches.

Standing Stone, 1989. 48 x 13 x 13 inches.

Standing Stone, 1989. 48 x 13 x 13 inches.

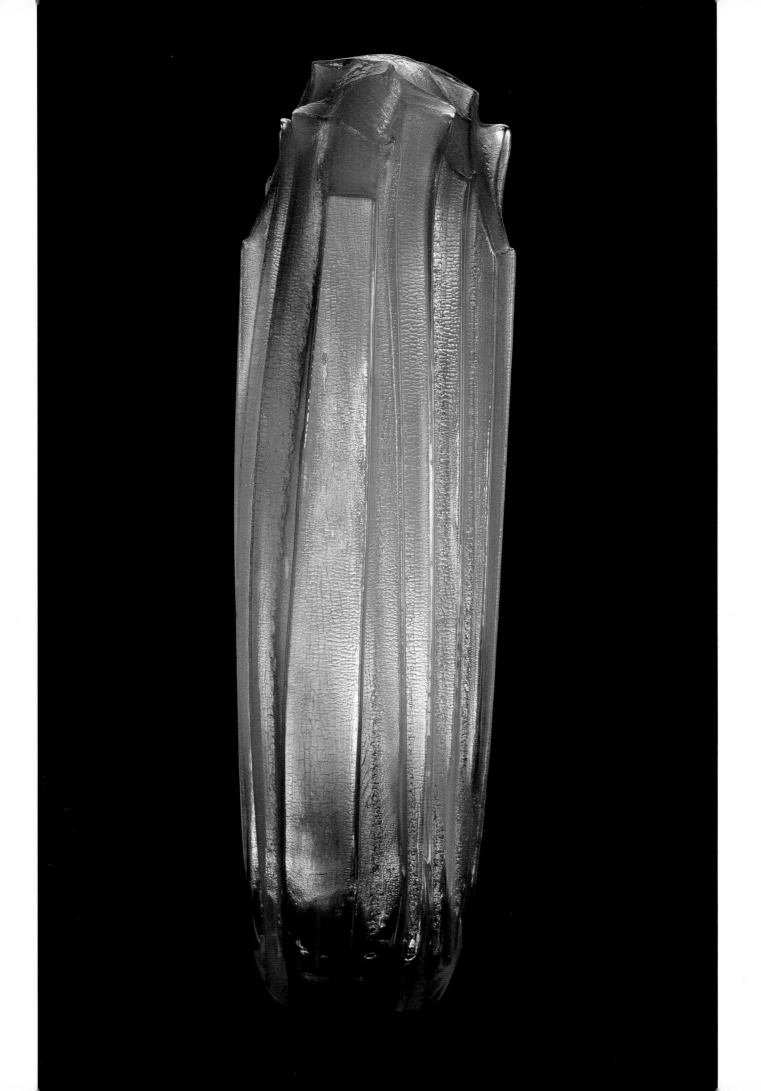

Morris at marver.

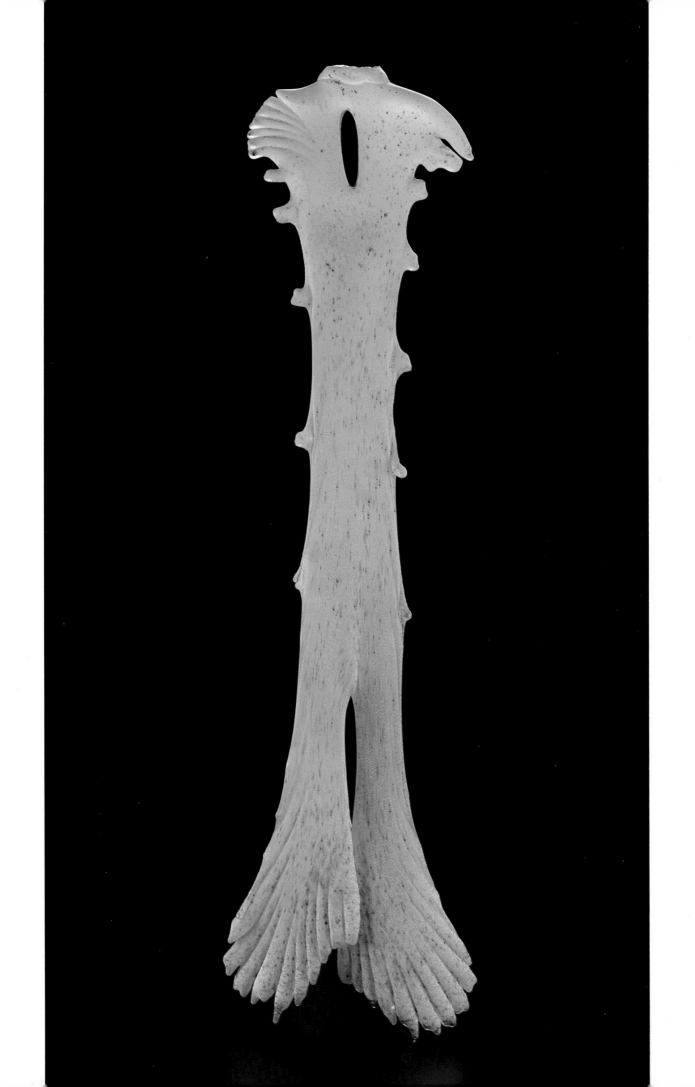

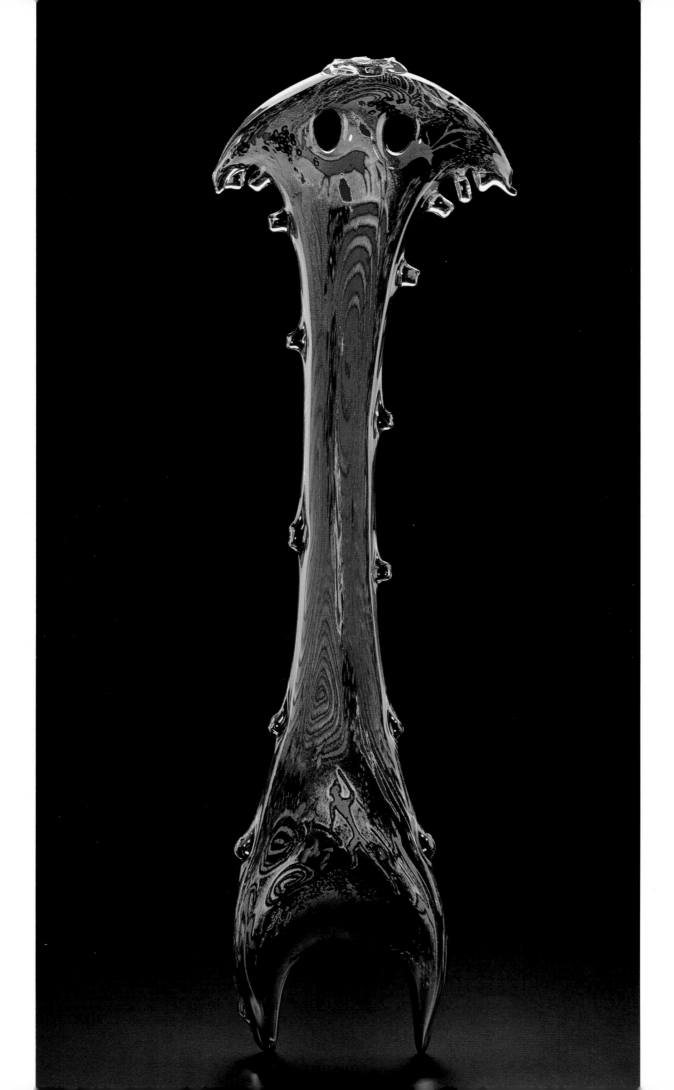

preceding pages:

Artifact (Baton), 1989. 46 x 11 x 3 inches.

Artifact (Baton), 1989. 48 x 12 x 9 inches.

Tusks, 1988. 12 x 36 x 28 inches.

Artifact Still Life, 1988.

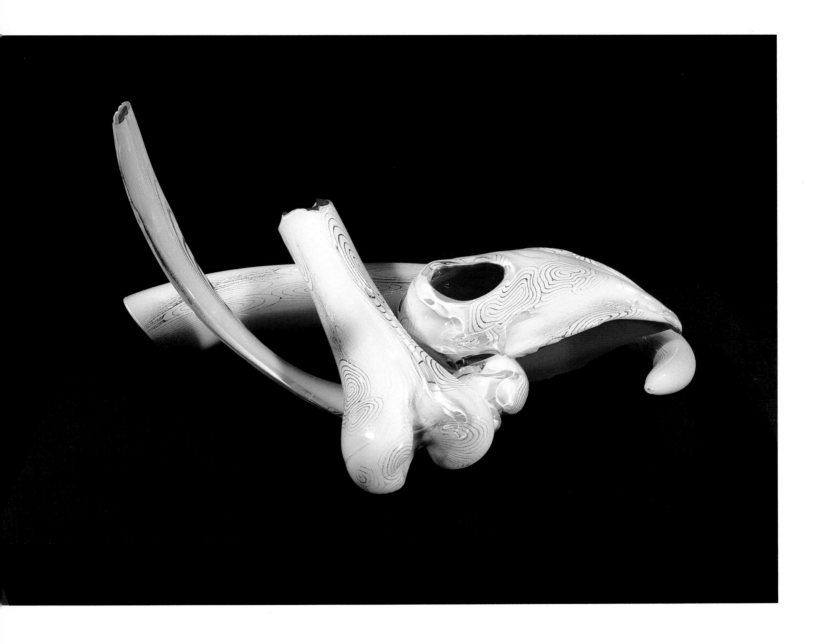

Artifact Still Life, 1988.

Tusk, 1988.

Pestle and Mortar Group, 1988. **Artifact Still Life, 1988.**

Tool Grouping, 1988.

Artifact Still Life, 1988.

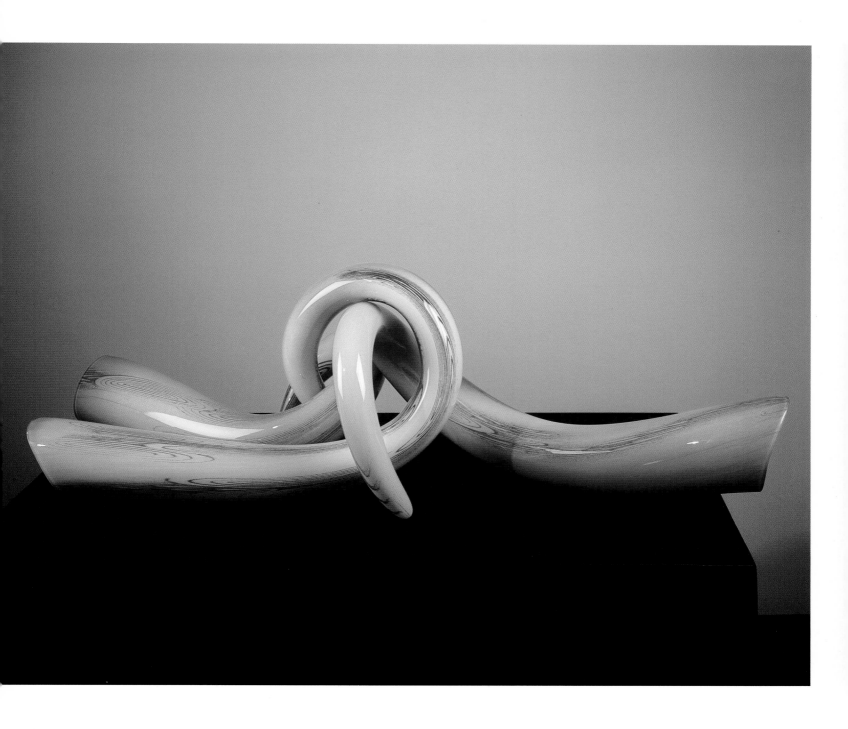

Tusks, 1988.

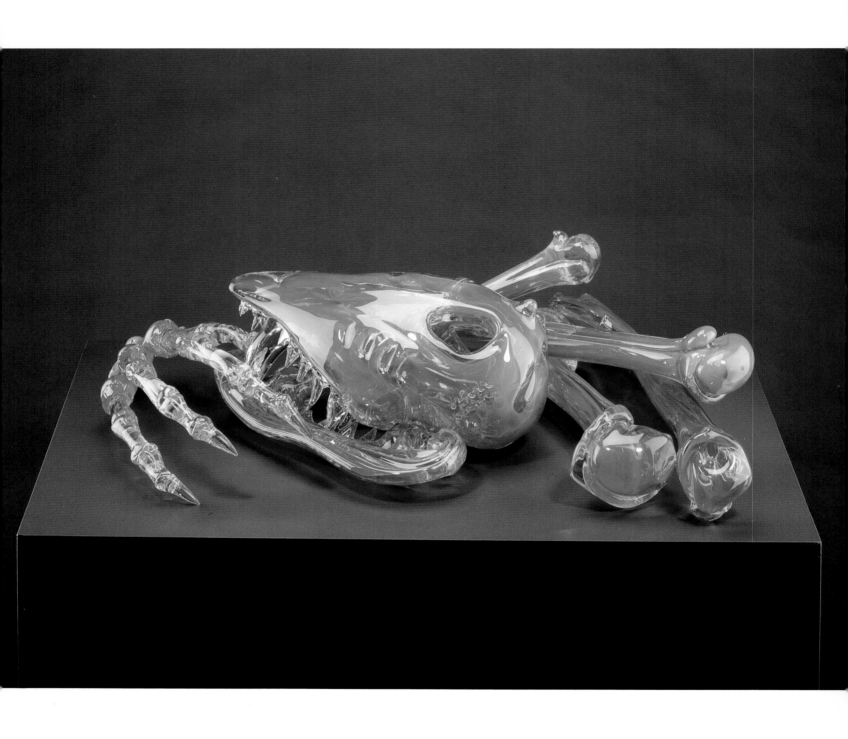

Artifact Series #3 (Hunter), 1988. 10 x 48 x 122 inches.

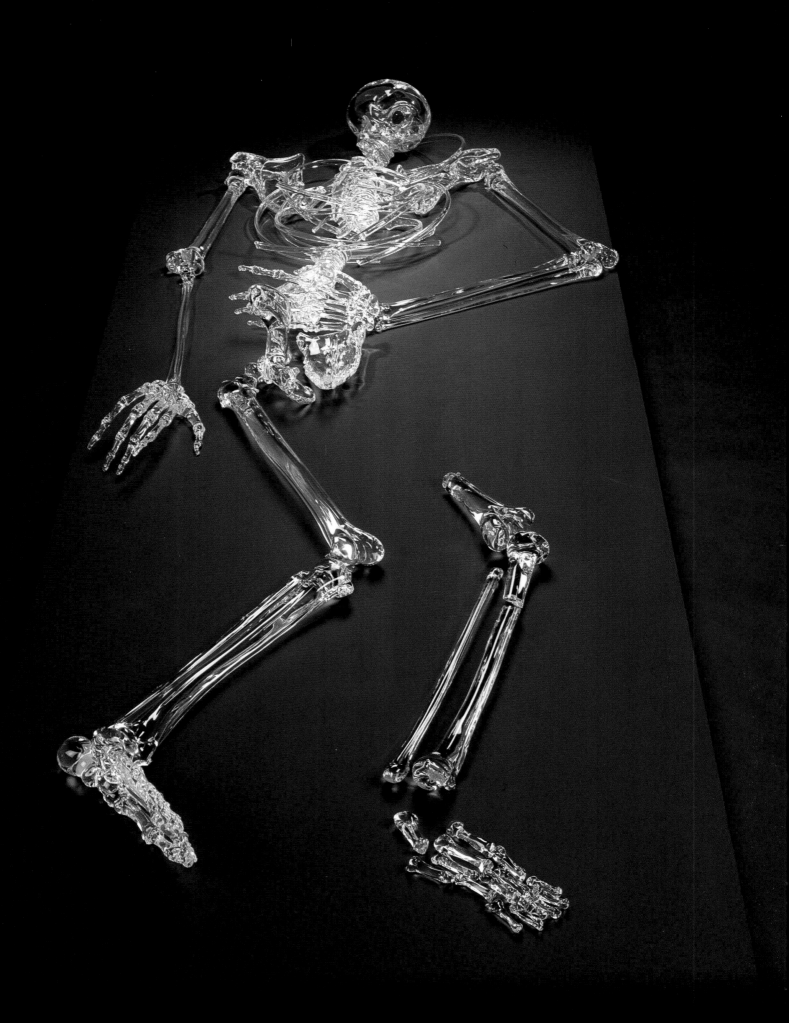

following pages:

Artifact Series #11 (Man and Beast), 1988. 18 x 108 x 60 inches.

Artifact Series #9 (Burial), 1989. 18 x 44 x 28 inches.

Artifact Series #6 (First Fruit), 1988. 12 x 84 x 48 inches.

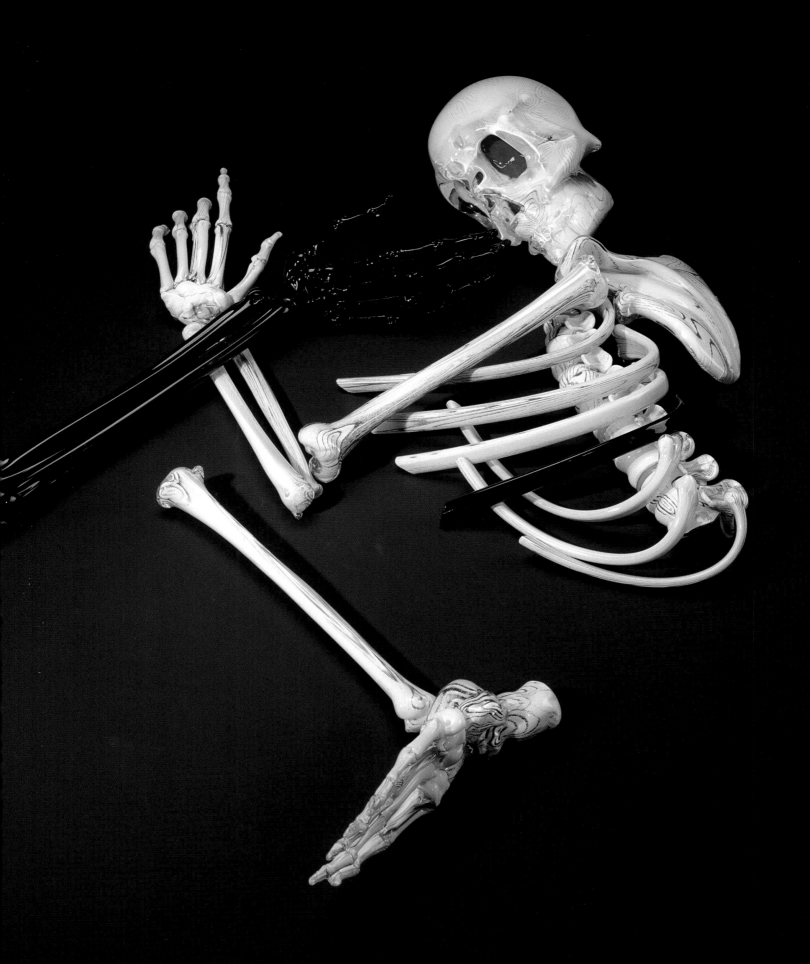

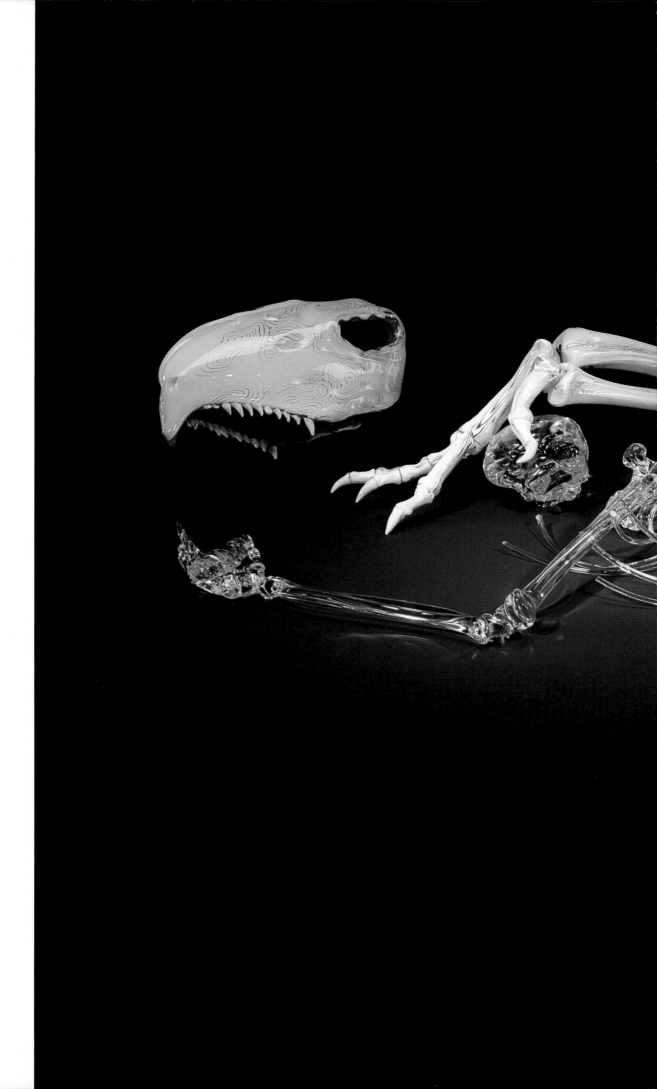

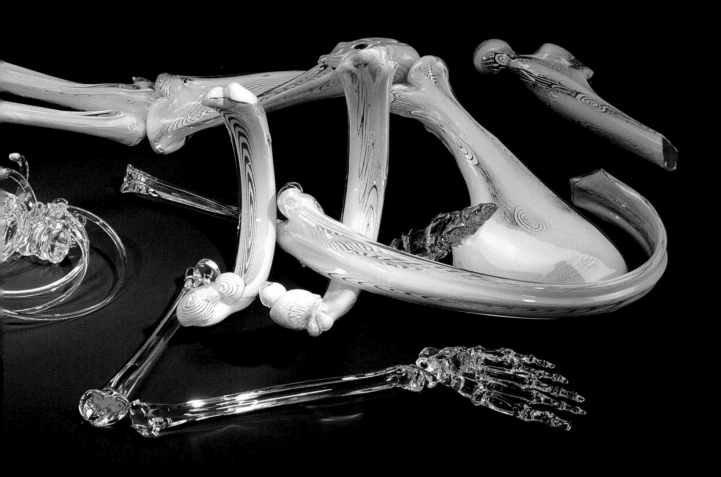

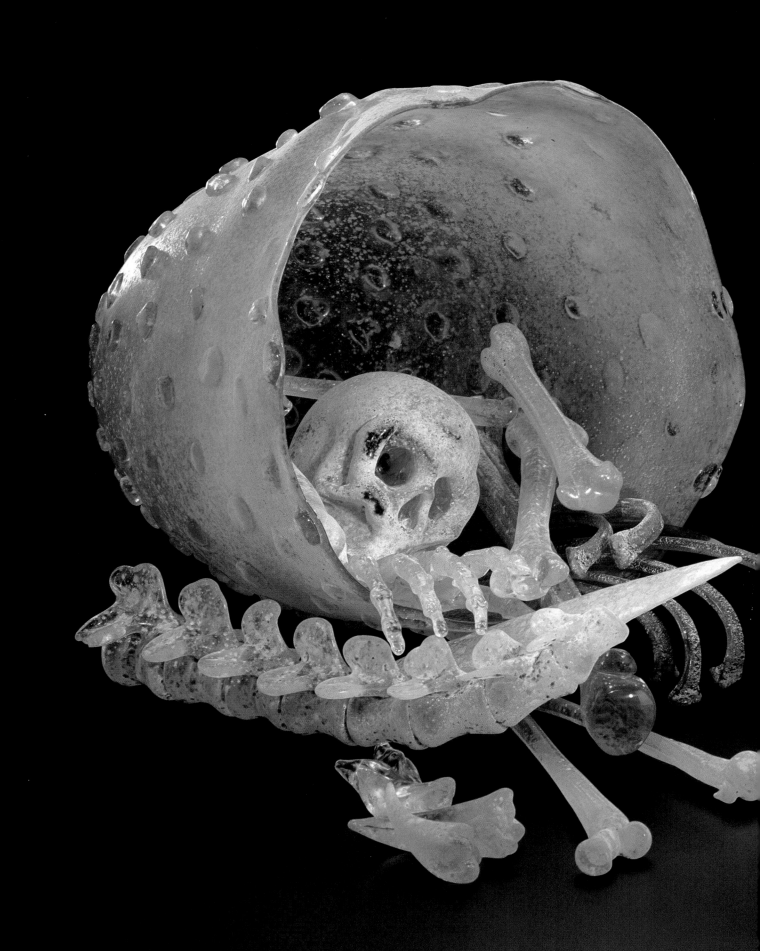

Artifact Series #14 (Offering), detail, 1989.

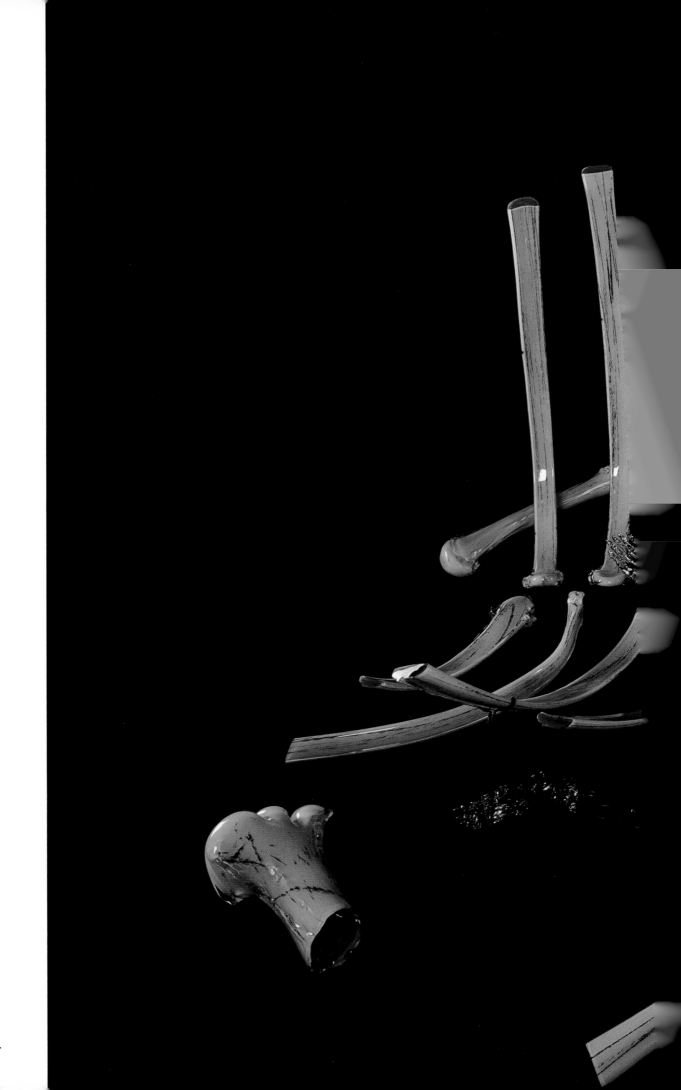

Artifact Series #14 (Offering), 1989.
96 x 120 x 120 inches.

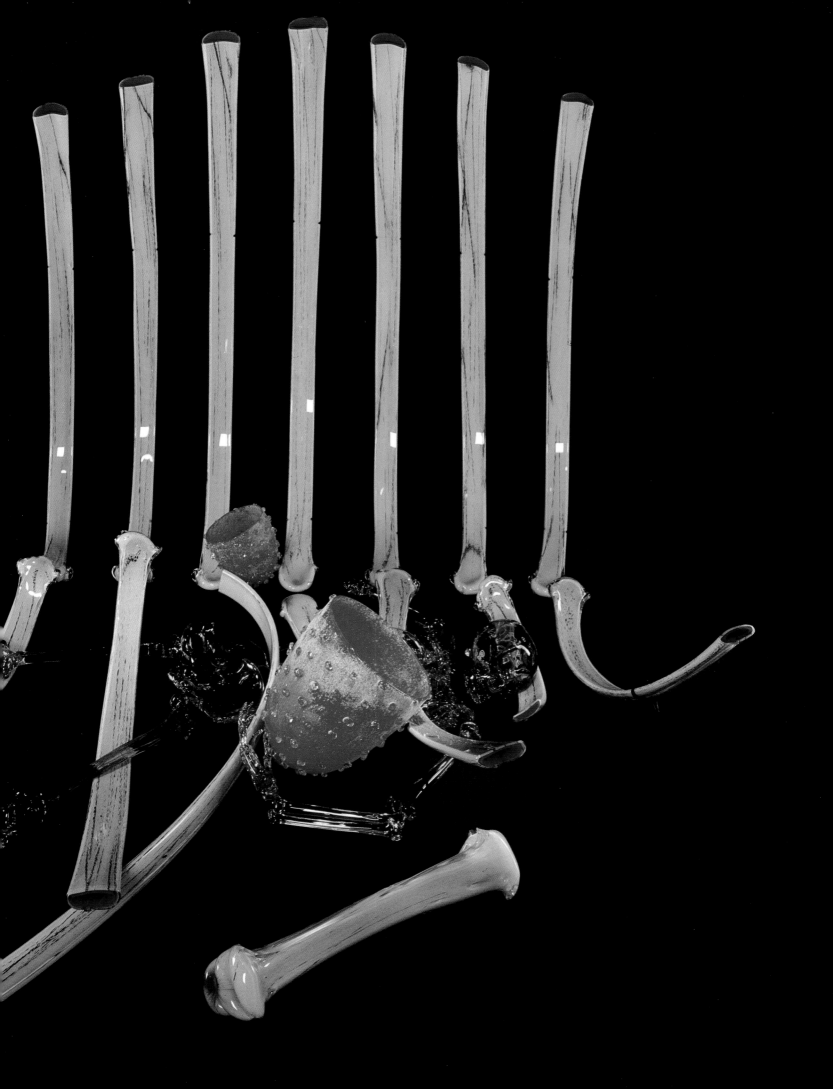

AFTERWORD

NARCISSUS QUAGLIATA

edited by
Brigid J. Guinan

on this page and the following pages:
Morris with assistants Jon Ormbrek, Paul DeSomma, and Jim Morris, working on Petroglyph Vessel and Standing Stone at the Pilchuck Glass School, Stanwood, Washington.

We experience William Morris's work with the same part of ourselves that responds to Stonehenge or any prehistoric site. Morris's work does not ask the viewer for an intellectual and studied response. It reaches and moves the viewer in a visceral way, stimulating a gut feeling, bypassing words, concepts, or thought.

William Morris strives to express with his forms a simplicity that has a timeless, universal appeal. He shies away from clearly identifiable cultural forms, contemporary or historical. He is not interested in following trends nor is he concerned with where his work fits in the present contemporary scene.

Using intuition as his guide, the artist enters a world of power, beyond culture, where nature is the primary mover to be feared and loved. He pursues images of a world that are primal, essential. Images of animals, hunters, bones, tools, and stones evoke a presence that is silent and eloquent.

Morris loves the outdoors and often hunts with a bow and arrow. Quiet and solitude appeal to him. Places like the Orkney Islands, where imposing megalithic stones stand silently on the moors, inspire him. Likewise rocks which have been washed by the sea into smooth and simple forms move Morris and influence his creations.

Glass itself also serves as a major inspiration for the artist. Morris believes that this stable, durable material which has been around for centuries has barely been explored. For Morris glass is in its infancy. His fascination with this viscous material and his relentless investigation of its properties fuel the success of his creations.

Morris first became intrigued by glass during his high school days in Carmel, California. He experimented with ceramics and glass while at California State University in Chico, and Central Washington University in Ellensburg. But his total immersion in the material occurred at the Pilchuck Glass School. The school was founded in 1971 by Dale Chihuly on land donated by John Hauberg and Anne Gould Hauberg. Located in the foothills of the Cascade Mountains north of Seattle, this center for the glass arts has been instrumental in

the renaissance of glass. Pilchuck has also been crucial to William Morris's development.

For eight years Morris blew on Dale Chihuly's team at Pilchuck. He developed his techniques and sensitivities within that atmosphere, improving year after year. He became acquainted with and learned from the many visiting faculty — working artists from all over the world who influenced and stimulated his desire to create his own world with this material. Morris honed his skills, traveling extensively through the United States, Canada, Europe, and New Zealand giving workshops and sharing and receiving information about his craft.

In his early twenties Morris found his own voice; it has been getting louder and clearer ever since. With nature and glass as his stimulus Morris introduces us to his world of monoliths or Standing Stones, vessels with petroglyphs, groupings of rock-like shapes, and his most recent glass sculptures, or Artifacts as he prefers to call them, resembling archaeological relics.

The surfaces of these works vary from shiny to matte, opaque to translucent, strong colors to muted grays. With certain works he leaves the task of making the statement to the form itself. Others have real images visible on surfaces that suggest ancient stones from a prehistoric age. Still others resemble petroglyphs with hunting and wildlife scenes. Animal and human figures are drawn as if by the same ancient hands that painted the caves at Lascaux. The blown vessel forms do not end up cylindrical, but are flattened in order to give the artist the space for the imagery. The vessel form becomes the canvas, a stage for the main event, which is the imagery itself. In the Standing Stone series the shapes are determined by the use of a wooden mold into which the artist blows the hot molten glass. These molds, which are quite amazing devices, are made by Morris's right-hand man and close friend, Jon Ormbrek.

THE DECORATIVE AND EXISTENTIAL ELEMENT

There is an interesting interplay between two aspects of William Morris's work. The work is existential in character, the vehicle for the artist's personal quest which is intense and meaningful. Yet it is also sensory and decorative. The surfaces are seductive. The colors are exquisite and engage us in the most superficial way. Upon seeing one of these pieces one's natural response is to want it.

There is a tension between these two aspects of the work. Even when the artist uses the most ominous imagery, the beauty that it radiates gives it an unusual feel. In each piece I sense the glass craftsman, whose instinct is to make beauty for its own sake, and the artist, whose effort is to invest the piece with vision and depth. The two merge, with each side vying to come out on top.

THE PETROGLYPHS

Morris's petroglyph drawings, primarily present on the surface of the vessels, are interpreted and laid out by Jon Ormbrek on a solid steel table with a heated surface. Using powdered glass, which appears much like sand, Ormbrek "draws" the image on the table and Morris then transfers it to the vessel.

The transferal of the drawing to the vessel occurs when the blown bubble is still in its preliminary cylindrical form. Morris takes this hot blown bubble and rolls it over the drawing. He then blows the vessel to its full size. The blowing process expands the glass and distorts the original drawing to give the piece its unique expression and character.

The landscape of the Orkney Islands has a bleak Nordic feel to it. The flat terrain contrasts strikingly with the monoliths erected in pre-Celtic times. These powerful, massive, natural geometric shapes make you wonder who erected the imposing blocks. William Morris was moved by the stones and also by the minds and energy of the people who placed them upright to make their statement — a statement which still stands today.

The atmosphere in which Morris's Standing Stones are made is reminiscent of a kind of primitive ritual. A team of five produces the work, with Morris in the lead handling the most demanding tasks. A charged intensity permeates the making of each piece. On the "pad," as the glassblowing studio is referred to, a loud stereo belts out a tune with strong rhythm. The beat helps keep the adrenaline going for the whole crew. With each gather of glass the piece grows bigger; as the glass is picked up and layered successively on the blowpipe, the intensity builds. The event peaks when Morris, who now has forty to sixty pounds of glass on the blowpipe, lowers the enormous bubble into the wooden mold. He then blows the glass hard to expand it and have it take on the geometric form by adhering to the negative shape of the mold.

Fire and smoke pour out in great quantity as the molten glass melds into and burns the wooden form. The heat is almost unbearable as Morris, Ormbrek, and the other three assistants disappear into the enveloping smoke. As this modern replay of a prehistoric ritual unfolds you feel that a mystery is being celebrated as each herculean effort is made by these craftsmen.

Few materials move the craftsman as deeply as hot glass. Molten glass glows with inner light. It's hypnotic and seductive to watch and it demands of the blower a conduct so precise, so in tune with the material's nature, that any slip will invariably result in failure.

I have seen and heard about so many gorgeous pieces almost fully formed, after hours of work, smash and shatter on the cement floor of the pad due to one wrong movement. Given a cycle of several days of work William Morris can at best claim a success ratio of

fifty percent of the pieces with this series. The others break or fail at some point during the process.

Initially the Standing Stones were entirely opaque, form and color being the key ingredients. As he continued with the series the stones became more translucent; light itself became an essential element. In contrast to the manner in which the Standing Stones are made, they feel "cool" when viewed in a gallery or museum. Of his productions they are the most sober.

THE ARTIFACTS

With this new series Morris's attention shifts from stones and ancient petroglyphs depicting animal and human figures to the very figures and "finds" themselves. The human figure becomes central, represented by its skeletal remains.

As a child in Carmel, Morris was always fascinated by the discovery and exploration of Indian burial grounds. These early forages influenced him deeply. Now he has found a way to integrate this fascination with his own work.

These works are not vessels that ride the ambiguous edge between art and craft. They are bold sculpture in glass. This direct and courageous approach brings William Morris to a new level closer to the core of his vision.

This series required that Morris learn how "to build" (as opposed to blow) sculptural forms. He went to Venice to watch and learn how the masters in Murano create those amazing glass statuettes of horse's heads, torsos, clowns and fishes. Morris absorbed their techniques, took the language home with him and gave it an extremely personal imprint. He created imagery that has power and depth.

For Morris death is not the subject of these remains from the distant past. In fact, it is not the remains themselves that interest Morris but the unanswered questions that these "situations" elicit. Each scene is a reality from his unconscious, an archetypal puzzle. A

skeleton has a point of a gold gilded crystal spear inside it. Another is white, juxtaposed with a black skeleton. Who was it that once lived and whose bones are these that survived? How did they live and how did death come to them?

The Artifacts appear fragile. A skeleton that survives thousands of years is already an awe-inspiring presence. When rendered in glass you heighten even more the sense of just how fragile existence really is. Like the light bones of birds the luminous and delicate glass bones make us feel just how tenuous and delicate our very bones can be.

The scale of the work is notable. Some are massive; one of his most recent works is an eight-by-ten-foot rib cage. As sculpture they engage the surrounding space in a more aggressive way. They do not sit so politely on their pedestals. They forcefully demand our attention. They make you think, feel, and wonder.

A MASTER CRAFTSMAN

William Morris would like to believe that his work escapes a clear cultural definition because he searches for a timeless place, a universal expression. But his passionate love for nature and its forms and his gutsy unintellectual approach reveal a West Coast upbringing. The craft movement of the last twenty years is the foundation on which he built his career. He expresses his thinking in doing and *that* is a typically California trait.

When I came from Europe to California I was taken by the fact that people did not like to sit around and talk about things forever. They just did them. That's where his work is and it represents the best that this cultural atmosphere creates.

Morris's work is exquisite, refined, and made with flawless techniques which he developed. Watching Morris work is a pleasure. I have never seen a craftsman so totally at one with the material he uses. He admits his ability is rooted in his facility to totally concentrate. While working his movements are economical and precise. They flow with the nature of the material.

   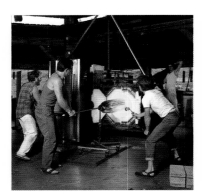

With each piece the artist challenges himself and fine tunes his ability to work with the material. Never forcing it, he shapes it by intuitively guiding it in the direction he senses is right. "The glass wants to do this," he says. By giving the material the freedom to form itself he breathes life into it. To the untrained eye or the uninformed audience it might not be apparent that a great deal of William Morris's work is at the very edge of what is physically possible in glass.

Morris is intense about his work but probably would object to being called an artist. He thinks of himself as a craftsman pursuing what he loves to do. Labels such as "artist" make him feel uncomfortable and self-conscious. At the age of thirty-two, William Morris is perhaps the best American glass blower alive. Beyond that he has produced a body of work that is a statement. He is so young, with so much behind him, I cannot but wonder where he is going with his work and career.

The world he presents to us through his work is a vast expanse waiting to be explored. At this young age William Morris has more energy and focus than ever before. I'm looking forward to the depths he will reach as he continues his explorations and approaches his maturity.

LIST OF PLATES

Plates are listed according to page numbers. All photographs are by Robert Vinnedge Photography, Seattle, unless otherwise noted.

2/3. Installation, Brendan Walter Gallery, 1988. Foreground: collection of Jennifer Naimy and Robert Raphael. Photograph by Winthrop Brookhouse.

6. Petroglyph Vessel, detail, 1988.

8. Artifact Series #3 (Hunter), detail, 1988. See page 67.

14/15. Roundel and Vessels with shard drawings, 1979. Private Collection. Photographs by Ira Garber.

17. Stone Vessel, 1984. 12 x 15 x 4½ inches. Collection of the artist.

18. Stone Vessel and Standing Stone, 1984. Collection of Missoula Museum of the Arts, Montana.

19. Stone Vessel, 1984. Private Collection.

20. Stone Vessels, 1984–1986. 15 to 20 inches high. Clockwise from upper left: collection of Gloria and Sonny Kamm; collection of the artist; collection of Mr. and Mrs. Lee Hills; private collection.

21. Stone Vessels, 1984–1986. 15 to 20 inches high. Clockwise from upper left: private collection; collection of David Esoldi; private collection; collection of the artist.

22/23. Standing Stone and Stone Vessel, detail, left, 1985. Collection of Dr. and Mrs. Norman Stone.

24. Petroglyph Vessel, 1985. Collection of Mr. and Mrs. Adam Aronson.

25. Standing Stone, 1985. Collection of the artist. Petroglyph Vessel, reverse side of page 24.

26/27. Petroglyph Vessel (Fighting Elks), detail left, 1988. Private collection.

28/29. Petroglyph Vessel, 1988. 21 x 19 x 4½ inches. Both sides. Collection of the artist.

30. Petroglyph Vessel, 1988. 20 x 17 x 5 inches. Collection of Gilmore, Aafedt, Forde, Anderson and Gray, P.A.

31. Petroglyph Vessels, 1988. Collection of the artist.

32/33. Petroglyph Vessel, 1988. Both sides. Collection of Paul Brainerd.

34/35. Petroglyph Vessel, 1988. Both sides. Collection of Donald Foster.

39. Standing Stone and Rocks, 1986. 33 x 30 x 24 inches. Collection of the artist.

40. Rocks, 1986. Private collection.

41. Vessel and Rocks, 1988. 21 x 36 x 30 inches. Collection of Jeremy Burdge.

42. Standing Stone, 1983. Collection of the artist.

43. Standing Stone, 1984. Collection of the artist.

44. Rocks, 1987. 8 x 28 x 22 inches. Collection of the artist.

45. Vessel and Rocks, 1988. Courtesy of Brendan Walter Gallery.

46. Standing Stone, 1985. Collection of the artist.

47. Standing Stones, 1987. Collection of Harvey K. Littleton (left), collection of the artist (right).

48. Standing Stone with Petroglyphs, 1987. Collection of Robert Vinnedge.

49. Standing Stone, 1989. Collection of the artist.

50. Standing Stone, 1989. Collection of the artist.

51. Standing Stone, 1989. 48 x 13 x 13 inches. Collection of the artist.

54. Artifact (Baton), 1989. 46 x 11 x 3 inches. Collection of the artist.

55. Artifact (Baton), 1989. 48 x 12 x 9 inches. Collection of the artist.

56. Tusks, 1988. 12 x 36 x 28 inches. Collection of the artist.

57. Artifact Still Life, 1988. Collection of Dr. Earl M. Van Sandt.

58. Artifact Still Life, 1988. Courtesy of Brendan Walter Gallery.

59. Tusk, 1988. Courtesy of Brendan Walter Gallery. Photograph by Winthrop Brookhouse.

60. Pestle and Mortar Group, 1988. Collection of the artist.

61. Artifact Still Life, 1988. Collection of the artist.

62. Tool Grouping, 1988. Collection of Richard Bogonolmy.

63. Artifact Still Life, 1988. Collection of Mimi Livingston.

64. Tusks, 1988. Courtesy of Brendan Walter Gallery. Photograph by Winthrop Brookhouse.

65. Artifact Series (Himself to Himself), 1988. Collection of the artist.

67. Artifact Series #3 (Hunter), 1988. 10 x 48 x 122 inches. Collection of the artist.

68/69. Artifact Series #6 (First Fruit), 1988. 12 x 84 x 48 inches. Collection of the artist.

70/71. Artifact Series #11 (Man and Beast), 1988. 18 x 108 x 60 inches. Collection of the artist.

72/73. Artifact Series #9 (Burial), 1989. 18 x 44 x 28 inches.

75. Artifact Series #14 (Offering), detail, 1989.

76/77. Artifact Series #14 (Offering), 1989. 96 x 120 x 120 inches. The Prescott Collection of Pilchuck Glass at Pacific First Centre, Seattle.

SELECTED PUBLIC COLLECTIONS

American Craft Museum, New York

American Glass Museum, Millville, New Jersey

Auckland Museum, Auckland, New Zealand

Corning Museum of Glass, Corning, New York

Delta Airlines, Portland, Oregon

First Union Bank, Charlotte, North Carolina

Hokkaido Museum of Modern Art, Hokkaido, Japan

IBM Corporation, Tulsa, Oklahoma

J.B. Speed Art Museum, Louisville, Kentucky

Joslyn Art Museum, Omaha, Nebraska

Los Angeles County Museum of Art, California

McDonald's Corporation, Bellevue, Washington, and Oak Park, Illinois

Missoula Museum of the Arts, Missoula, Montana

Musée des Arts Décoratifs, Paris

Museum für Kunst und Gewerbe, Hamburg, West Germany

Museum of Art, Rhode Island School of Design, Providence, Rhode Island

Pilchuck Collection, Stanwood, Washington

Port of Seattle, Washington

Prescott Collection of Pilchuck Glass at Pacific First Centre, Seattle, Washington

Rockefeller Center, New York

Royal College of Art, London

Safeco Corporation, Seattle, Washington

Seafirst Bank Collection, Seattle, Washington

Seattle Repertory Theatre, Seattle, Washington

Security Pacific Bank, Seattle, Washington

Sheldon Memorial Art Gallery, University of Nebraska, Lincoln

Sheraton Collection, Boston and Seattle

Shimonosedi Museum, Hokkaido, Japan

United Airlines, San Francisco

University of Michigan, Dearborn

U.S. News and World Report, Washington, D.C.

Valley National Bank, Tucson and Phoenix, Arizona

Victoria and Albert Museum, London

Virginia Museum of Fine Arts, Richmond

Westin Hotel, San Francisco

William Morris and Jon Ormbrek, Cascade Mountains. Photograph by Paul DeSomma

ACKNOWLEDGMENTS

I would like to recognize the individuals and institutions which have made this work possible:

my family for their spiritual support;

all of the assistants who have helped in the making of the pieces;

the Pilchuck Glass School for providing opportunity and place;

and special thanks to Dale Chihuly for guidance as friend and mentor.

My deepest gratitude goes to my friend Jon Ormbrek who, for thirteen years, has been invaluable in the development of all facets of the work.

WM